Music Minus One Trombone

CLASSIC STANDARDS
for Trombone

mmo
3995
Vol. 2

T0056207

Music Minus One Trombone

CLASSIC STANDARDS
for Trombone

CONTENTS

All songs transcribed and engraved by Robert Edwards

ISBN 978-1-941566-82-4

MMO 3995

How Little We Know

Words and music by Carolyn Leigh and Philip Springer

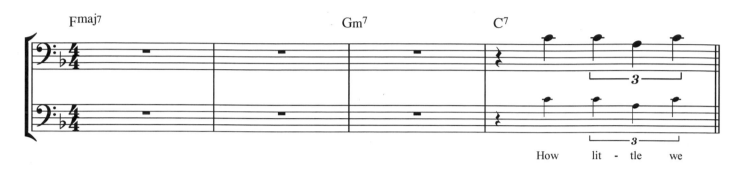

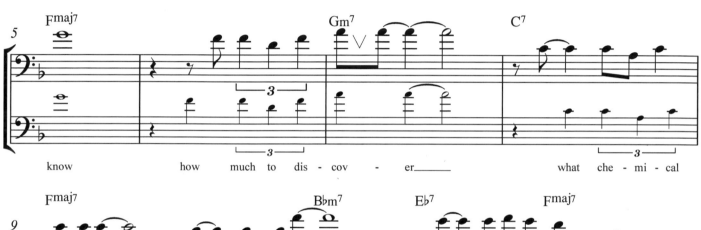

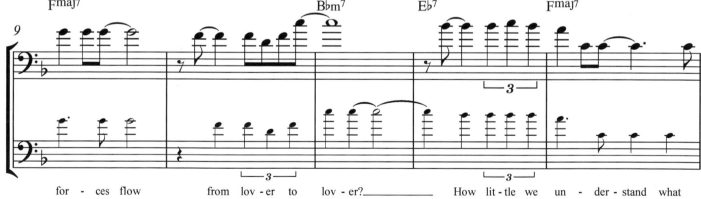

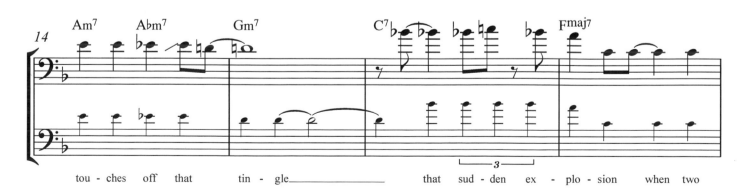

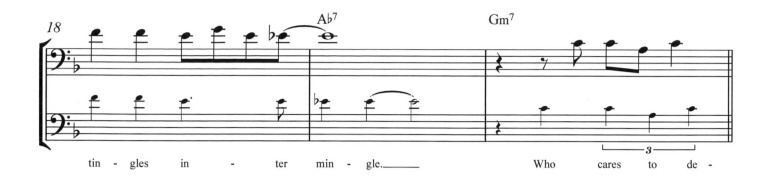

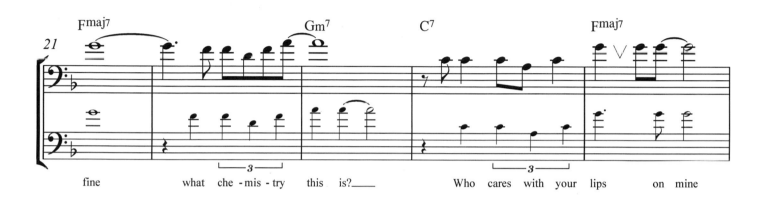

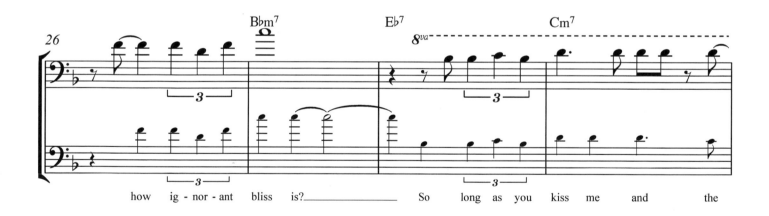

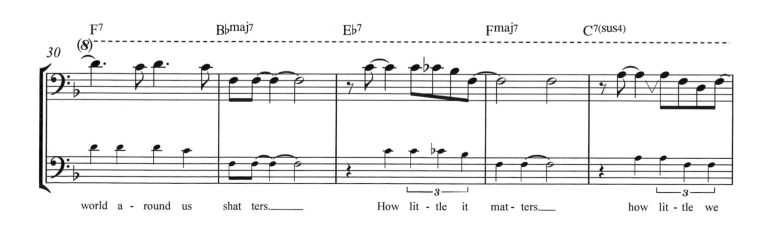

MMO 3995

6

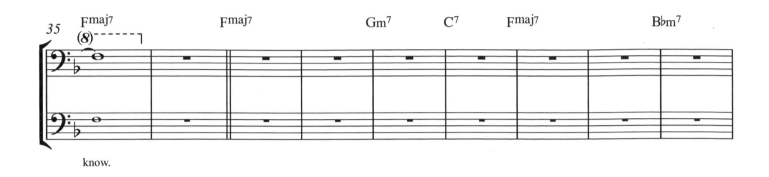

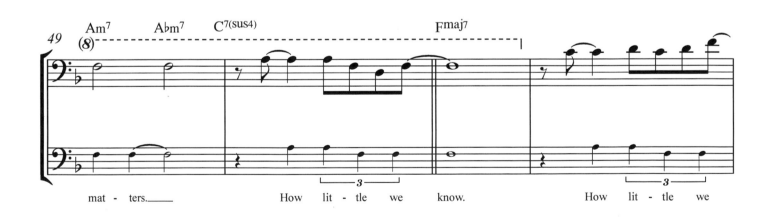

Where Are You?

Words and music by
Harold Adamson and Jimmy McHugh

Fools Rush In

Words and music by
Johnny Mercer and Rube Bloom

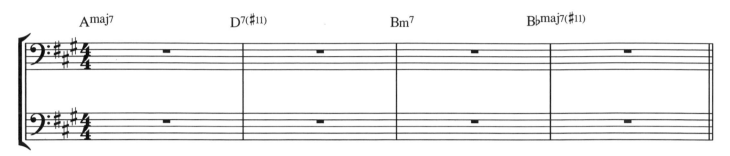

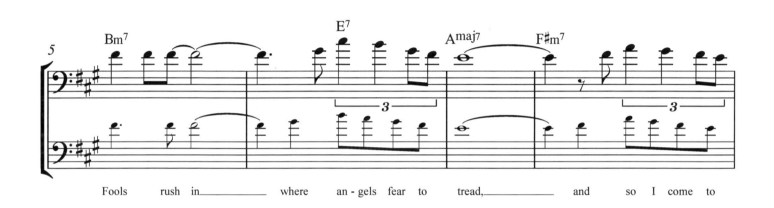

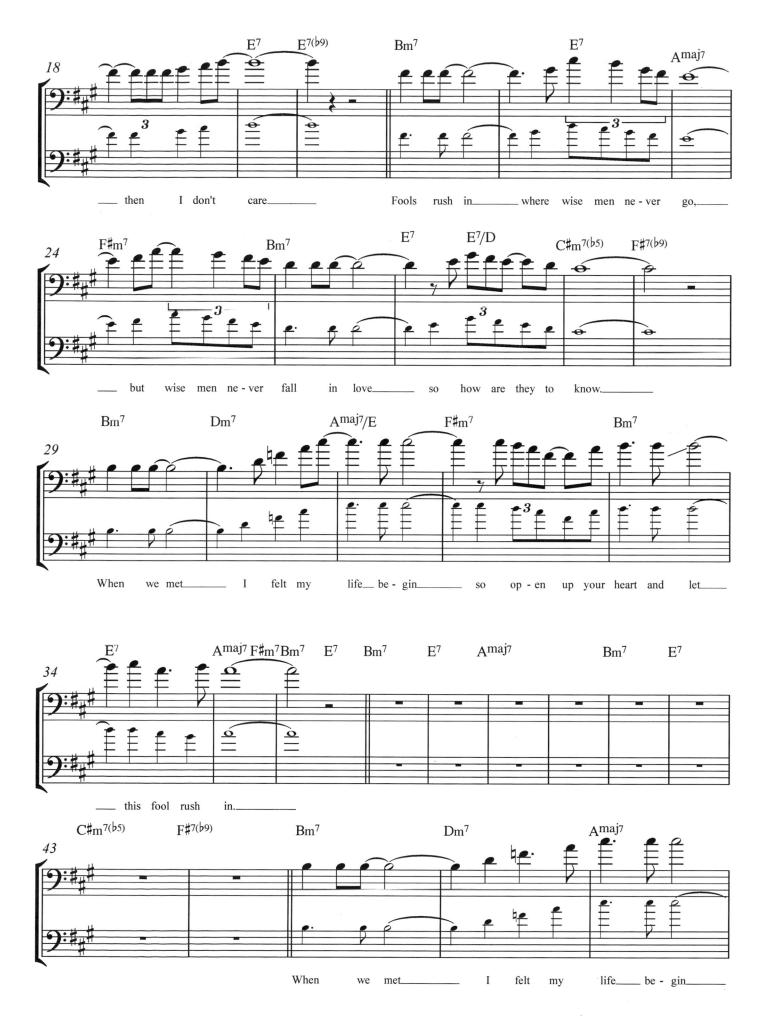

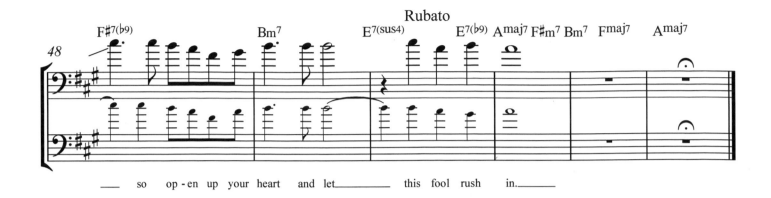

_____ so op-en up your heart and let_____ this fool rush in._____

Fly Me To The Moon

Words and music by Bart Howard

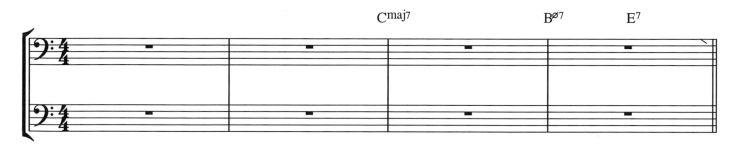

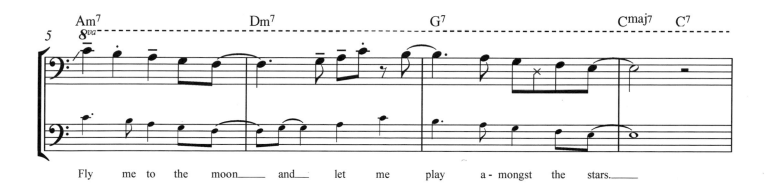

Fly me to the moon___ and___ let me play a - mongst the stars.___

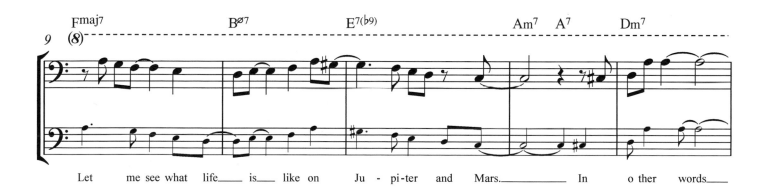

Let me see what life___ is___ like on Ju - pi-ter and Mars.___ In o ther words___

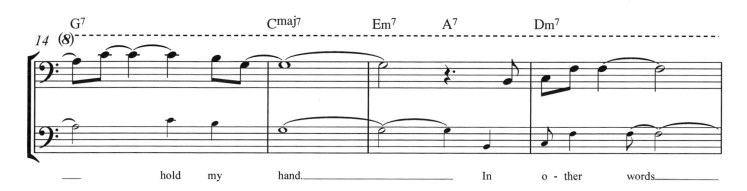

___ hold my hand.___ In o - ther words___

Palm Valley Music, LLC. (ASCAP)c/o The Richmond Organization2
66 West 37th Street, 17th FloorNew York, NY 10018

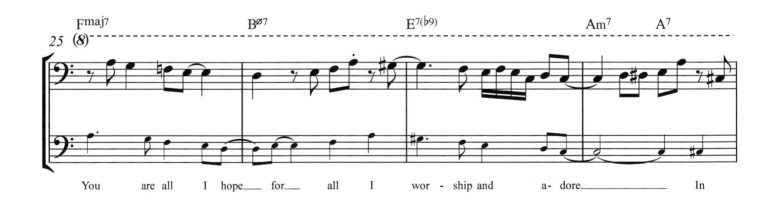

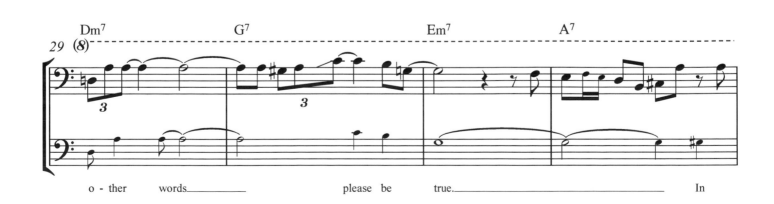

o - ther   words_____   I   love   you.

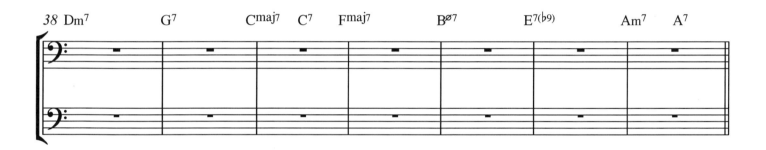

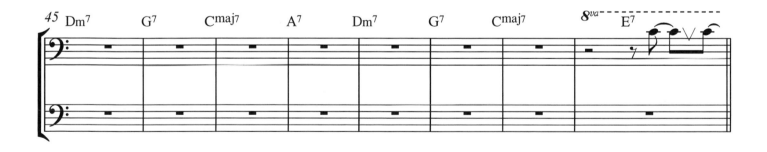

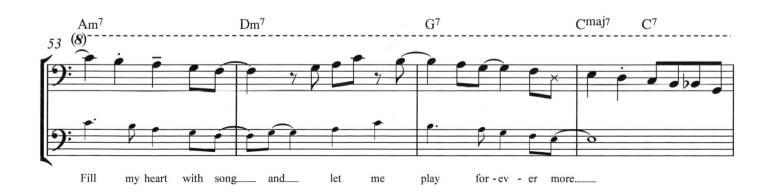

Fill   my heart   with   song____ and____   let   me   play   for - ev - er   more.____

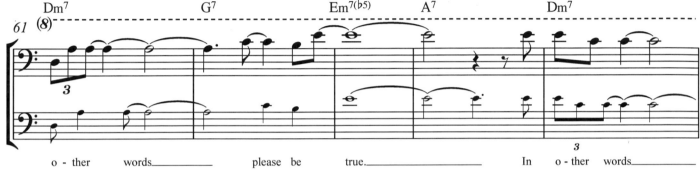

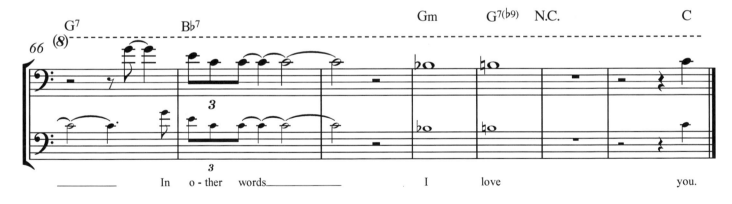

I Get Along Without You Very Well

Words and music by Hoagy Carmichael

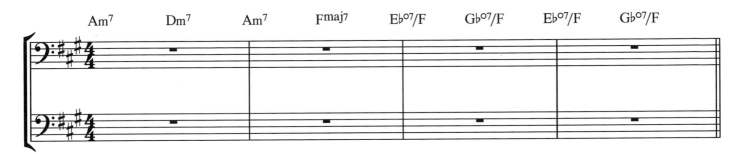

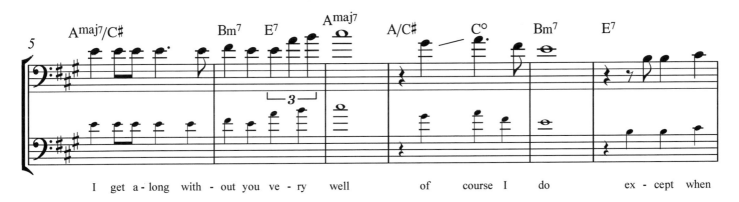

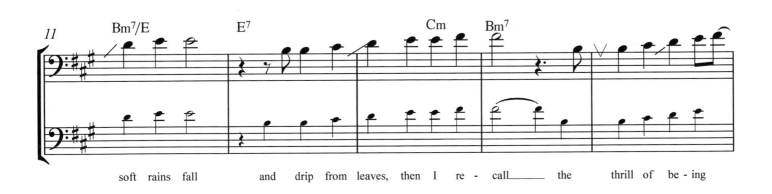

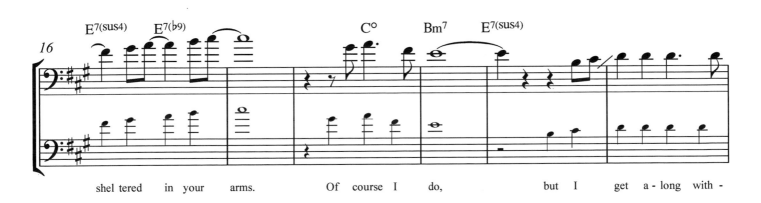

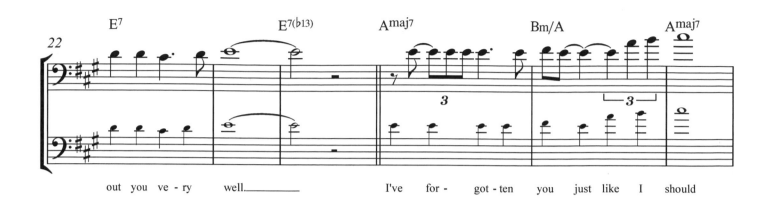

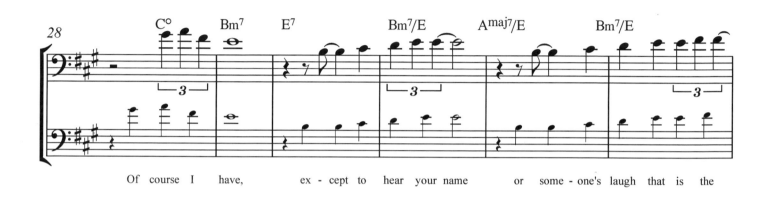

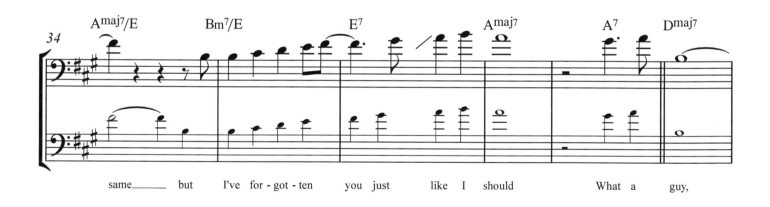

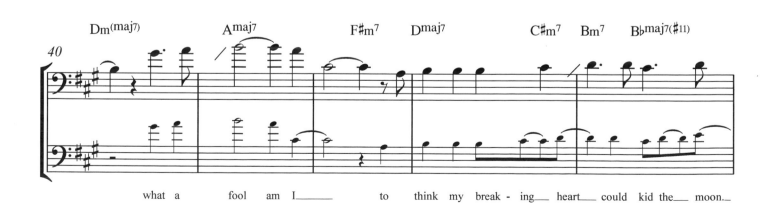

19

MMO 3995

Wave

Words and music by Antonio Carlos Jobim

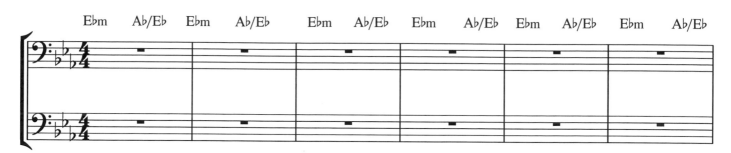

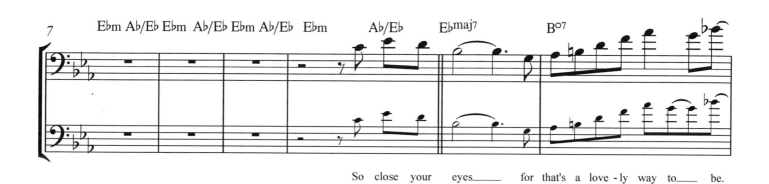

So close your eyes___ for that's a love - ly way to___ be.

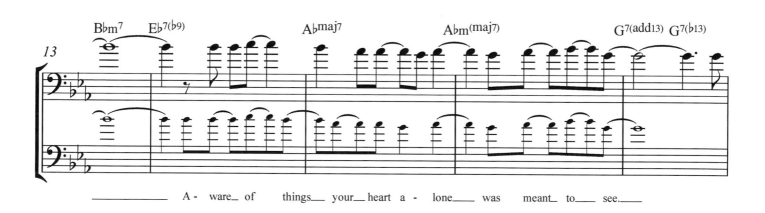

_____ A - ware__ of things__ your__ heart a - lone__ was meant to__ see.___

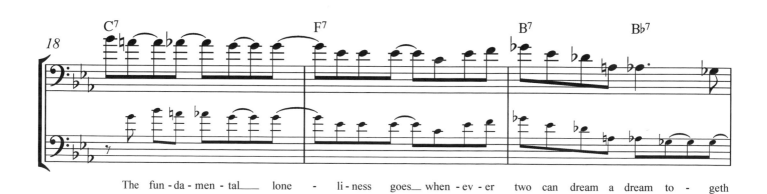

The fun - da - men - tal__ lone - li - ness goes__ when - ev - er two can dream a dream to - geth

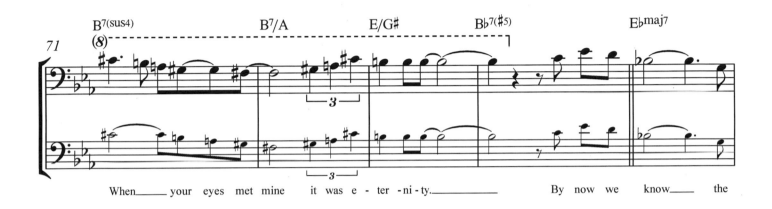

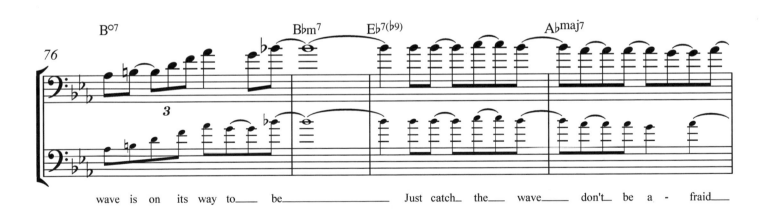

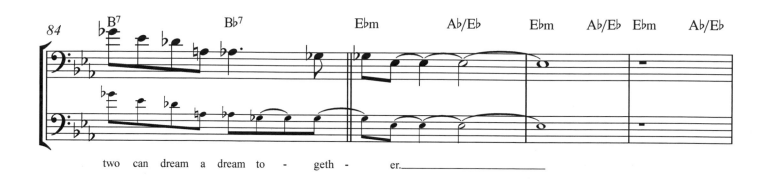

two can dream a dream to - geth - er._____

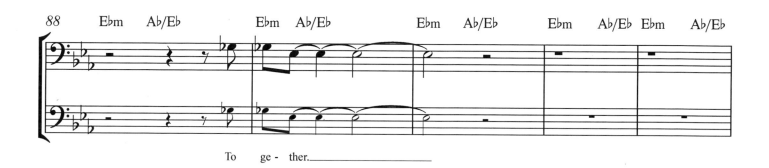

To ge - ther._____

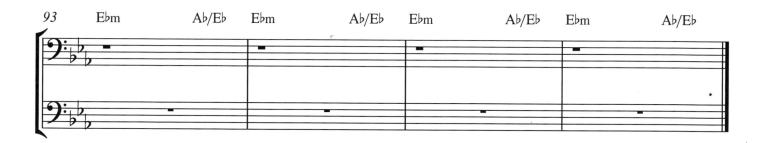

September Song

Words and music by
Maxwell Anderson and Kurt Weill

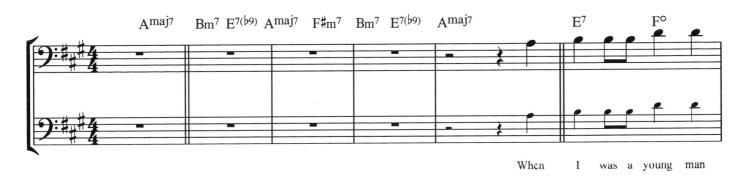

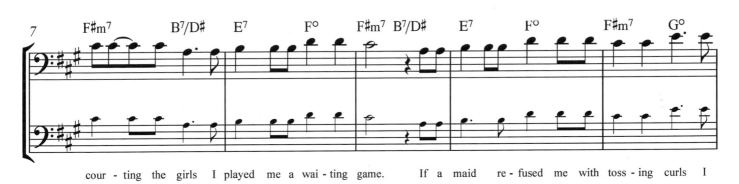

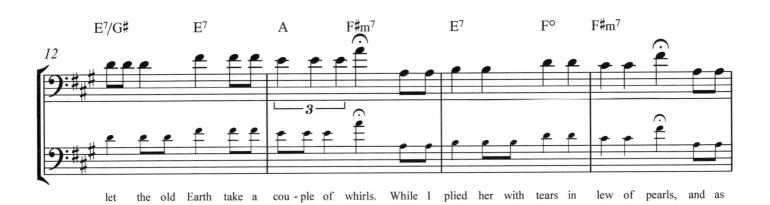

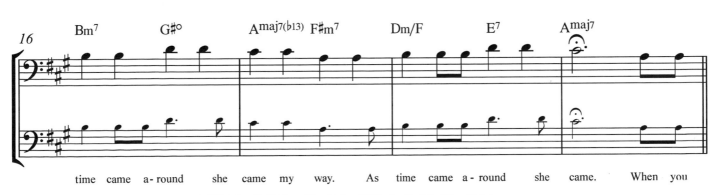

Almost Like Being In Love

Words and music by
Alan Jay Lerner and Frederick Loewe

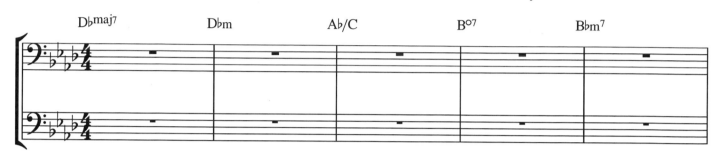

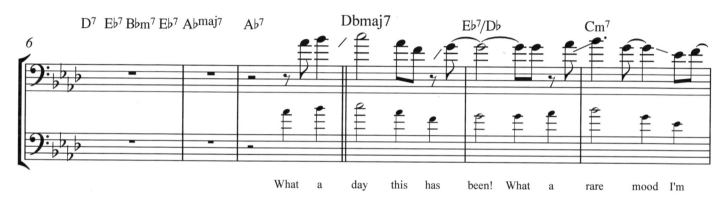

What a day this has been! What a rare mood I'm

in! Why, it's al - most like be - ing___ in love. There's a smile on my

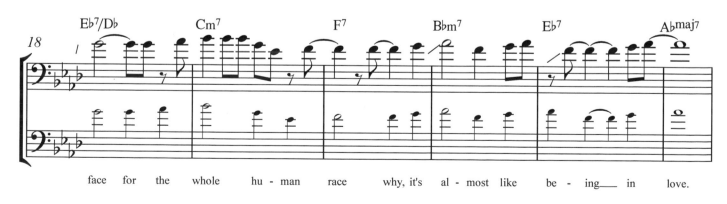

face for the whole hu - man race why, it's al - most like be - ing___ in love.

The Nearness of You

Words and music by
Ned Washington and Hoagy Carmichael

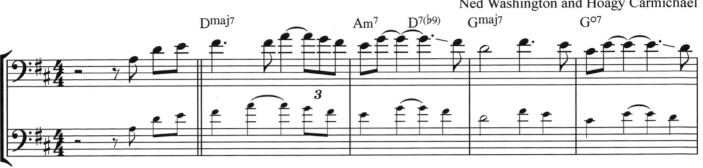

It's not the pale moon___ that ex - cites me___ that thrills and de - lites me___ oh

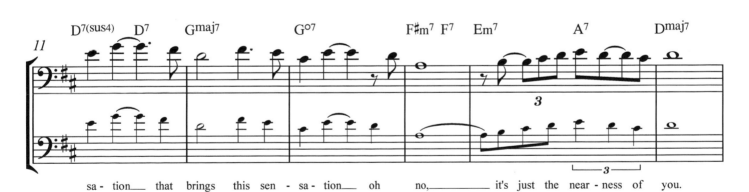

no,_____ it's just the near - ness of you. It is - n't your sweet___ con - ver -

sa - tion___ that brings this sen - sa - tion___ oh no,_____ it's just the near - ness of you.

When you're in my arms_____ and I feel you___ so close to me_____ all___ my

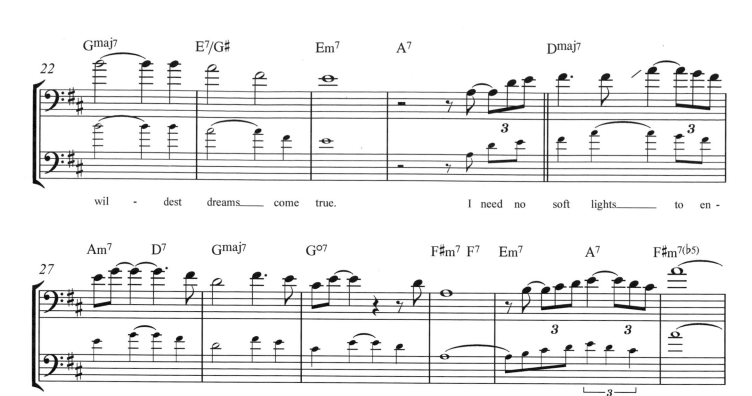

wil - dest dreams___ come true. I need no soft lights___ to en-

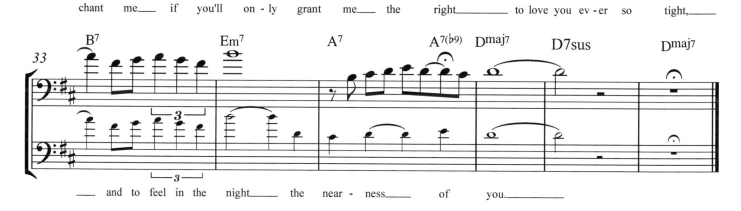

chant me___ if you'll on-ly grant me___ the right___ to love you ev-er so tight,___

and to feel in the night___ the near-ness___ of you.___

Music Minus One
50 Executive Boulevard • Elmsford, New York 10523-1325
914-592-1188 • e-mail: info@musicminusone.com
www.musicminusone.com

MMO 3995

ISBN 978-1-941566-82-4